MICHAEL

Mariah Whelan is an award-winning poet living in Oxfordshire, UK. She is the author of the novel-in-sonnets *the love i do to you* which was shortlisted for the Poetry Book Awards, the Melita Hume Prize and won the A M Heath Prize. She is the Jacqueline Bardsley Poet-in-Residence at Homerton College, The University of Cambridge, a Fellow in Creative Practice at University College London and one of the founding editors of *bath magg*, a magazine of the very best new poetry from UK and international poets.

Praise for *Michael*

Subversive in its tenderness, and fiercely original, *Michael* is a clear-eyed fable of post-Brexit Britain. Opening where hills rise above the bowl of a valley, at one remove from dreaming townspeople, its world is Aldi shops, damp gortex and mist, sandwich factory workers, pubs with Estonian football, demonstrating crowds. Loosely tethered to a mutually-bewildered father and daughter, but frequently voiced by an ironic, watery chorus, Mariah Whelan has created an extraordinary space of deep play. Mobile as the shifting weathers, bodies unspool into language, or interleave themselves through the sedimenting of memory. Lyrical, heart-catching, and relentlessly inventive, *Michael* is an unmissable and thrilling read.

— Alice Hiller, *Bird of Winter*

What's it like to haunt the life you're living now? If you could get outside of yourself would you like what you see? Can the words you impress upon your loved ones ever stand up to time? Mariah Whelan's *Michael* prompts these interrogations and more. At once garrulous and contemplative, this is a delicious reminder that the people we love are the most absurd and wonderful theatre we have.

— Rishi Dastidar, *Saffron Jack*

As the diachronic layers of slate once brought to light by Michael open to reveal the perfect black fern, so the voices of Whelan's chorus show the intimate nestled within the epic, and forge a vivid portrait of this squalid moment they emerge from: the vexed politics of / contemporary England / Brexit. Out of the things we can't fix, the words we don't strain to hear, Whelan crafts a harrowing work of breathtaking lyricism. From the chasm between generations Whelan mines questions of inheritance, memory and the sublimely dangerous and divisive power of language.

— Nancy Campbell, *The Library of Ice*

Michael is a text to place into the hands of anyone whole cares about poetry, about the state of the country, about the nature of language. It is a text for anyone who feels. It is a text which came alive in my head, which created a whole theatrical immersive experience with no more than words on a page. It is a text which keeps growing and living beyond the limits of the page and your reading of it, which flows through you long after you have finished.

— Tom de Freston, *Wreck*

Michael

Mariah Whelan

Also by Mariah Whelan

the rafters were still burning.   (Dancing Girl Press, 2021)

the love i do to you   (Eyewear, 2019)

ISBN: 978-1-915079-71-8

The author has asserted their right to be identified as the author of this Work in accordance with the Copyright, Designs and Patents Act 1988

Cover designed by Aaron Kent

Edited & Typeset by Aaron Kent

Broken Sleep Books Ltd
Rhydwen
Talgarreg
Ceredigion
SA44 4HB

Broken Sleep Books Ltd
Fair View
St Georges Road
Cornwall
PL26 7YH

Contents

SET

A small town in northern England. The town used to be a village but is now a place where people who don't want to live in the city but still work in the city buy new-build homes. One long street running through the town with two charity shops, a Co-Op, a good number of TO LET signs and a thriving Costa. Little cobbled streets running off the long road down the hill into a valley with a stream splashing through it. Little cobbled streets running up the hill that branch into cul-de-sacs of new developments. A mill with blown-out windows in the town centre surrounded by barbed wire. Night. Rain.

DRAMATIS PERSONAE

The Townspeople – mostly asleep with rain pattering on their windows
The Chorus – eight voices who haunt the town and move like water
Michael – an old man asleep on the moor above the town

Act One, Scene One: Night

[*Lights up on the town already on stage holding its breath. Townspeople asleep in their beds etc. Chorus enter like fog climbing out of manholes.*]

Voices [together]: We are a chorus that moves like water

Voice 1: Daytimes we drizzle over playgrounds

Voice 5: and down the common

Voice 6: We get into hills

Voices [together]: We soak through ground

Voice 1: drain through the water table

Voice 5: coming up again in butler sinks

                                                       Voice 2: and toilet bowls

Voice 6: At night we drip through holes in human dreams

Voice 1: tune through sleeping heads

                                        Voice 3: like a radio through stations

Voice 6: In stone houses and the council flats

                                              Voice 3: we seep like water

Voice 1: watching dreams play out

Voice 6: across closed lids

                                        Voice 7: And why watch?

Voices [together]: What else is there to do?

                                        Voice 2: There's *literally* nothing else to do

Voice 1: but dribble through clean dreams of a vicar in his bed

Voice 6: or condense on long walls

Voice 5: in rooms above the sandwich factory

Voice 1: where men sleep two-to-a-pillow

Voice 5: dreaming Romanian dreams

Voice 7: We watch

Voices [together]: and that's all you need to know

Voice 6: And who is this asleep above the town

Voice 6: in a tent of wet nylon

Voice 1: where the moor meets farmland?

Voice 1: Their mind is quiet inside their skull

Voice 3: like the layer of cold water

Voice 7: at the bottom of a pond

Voice 5: What washes up on the shoreline of his dreams?

Voice 2: If you can call it a shoreline

Voice 7: Call it an edge then

Voice 1: Yes call it reeds

Voice 4: A name

Voice 1: What name?

Voice 4: Michael

Voice 5: Anything else?

Voice 4: a sister a daughter a kingdom

Voice 2: coke tins crisp packets

Voice 4 [channelling Michael]: *You know where you are with a mountain*

Voice 1: What's that?

Voice 4: *All things can be measured, maintained*

Voice 5: Shh, listen!

Voice 4: *The trick to raising a girl is*

Voice 5: Tell us Michael!

Voice 4: *to treat them the same as a boy*

Voice 6: Wait a second—

Voice 2: What?

Voice 5: Play that bit again

Voice 6: Spool it back to its beginning

Voice 1: and let it play

Voice 4 [still channelling Michael]: Water wakes me. Raindrops on nylon, dripping off the Douglas firs, twanging the guy ropes. I eat breakfast in the tent flap. Sausages, a soft white roll, watch the magpies pick through the car park. You know where you are with a mountain (I pack up the tent pegs, telescopic poles, knee out the groundsheet the best I can). I'm not interested in the high peak anymore. I take the

Voice 8: Press your face up to the glass walls of Michael's dream

Voice 7: What do you see?

Voice 1: A hand shielding blue eyes

farm tracks up to where the fields give out to rougher ground, a bit of gorse and then it's red ferns far as the horizon. I keep my map in a plastic wallet. I know the way, more or less, but in this rain the path's half beck-bed and new streams cut in across the ferns. You can't trust the sound of water.

Voice 3: A man pressing out of a thicket of Horse Tails

Voice 5: His face holds a day's worth of grey stubble

I've read that many maps, sometimes I think I see the contour lines. Twenty-five, thirty, thirty-five yards, a steep run of brown loops tailing off into the flat tops, the softer sedimentary rock worn off by ice and rain. It's like reading, walking this valley. It's like reading a book—proper, old history—right here trodden into the ground. Sheep keeping the grass low on the midden pits and earthworks, ironstone wearing through the soil and the magnetism keeping it all together. That's the only thing that will save you in zero visibility. When the clouds come in (which they do) and the world is my hood, hands and gortex sleeves, I take out my compass and go way-point to way-point. You can get anywhere you want like that. I go off the path, first thing, before other folk can be bothered getting up. There's a wood down there. An old one behind the pines where the trees have beards and the lichen grows huge like two-penny pieces on the bark.

Voice 6: Damp hair pushed back from his forehead

Voice 5: Body carrying its small belly out in front of itself

Voice 6: Snug under his jacket zip

Voice 1: He presses out of a divot that marks the treeline

Voice 3: his left leg swinging forward

Voice 5: his right dragged to meet it

Voice 6: swing and step

Voice 5: swing and step

Voice 7: What's he doing out on the moor alone?

Voice 5: No mobile in his pocket

Voice 6: no GPS watch

Voice 2: An old git with something to prove

If you plan and have the right kit, most things can be managed. This weather's textbook. It's no freak storm, no bad luck, no iPhone that told you one thing and now here's another. It's just higher pressure on the hills, warm air forced up the valley to make those huge, black-bottomed cumulonimbi. That silver crack, that sunlight

Voice 8: Observe this man

Voice 7: and moment

Voice 8: Watch him walk through woods that line his dreams

12

behind the rain? I can practically see the iso-
bars. Look, there it is, coming up the slope. An
enormous invisible bouncing my breath back
at me, smeared and small, reduced to rain.

Voice 8: Watch him
speak to air
Voice 7: words
spooling out of his
mouth like tape
Voice 5: that cool
and harden in the
damp

Voice 7: What is
inside this tunnel of
language?
Voice 8: Tap it—

Voice 7: Listen to where the hollows are

Voice 1: under the surface of words

Voice 6: he fixes over his life as he walks

Voice 7: Under his thin cotton base layer

Voice 3: and the skin that laps like a seabed

Voice 7: where his muscles used to be

Voice 1: Look at the hot core of body he carries

Voice 6: up and out of this valley

Voice 1: wrapped in skin and Gortex

Voice 6: his buttocks and arms shrunk around the globe of his belly

Voice 5: with its coils of organs

Voice 8: Put your face up to the glass walls of his dream

Voice 7: watch it convulse

Voice 1: Watch the pocket of empty air he's just walked through

Voice 5: the wet grass holding imprints of his boots

Voice 6: for a moment

Voice 3: before they release back

Voices [together]: into pure grey dream

[Lights down on town. Chorus depart like rain]

Act One, Scene Two: Morning

[A room that looks out over the town. A bed in the centre of the room and a chair up-stage left turned towards the window. The sky in the window getting lighter like water diluting ink. An old woman in the chair, sleeping. The town stretches. Chorus enter like damp on bedsheets. Morning. Rain.]

Voice 1: Early morning we flush through storm drains

                                        Voice 3: and down-pipes

Voice 5: Cling to porcelain loos

Voice 6: fog blue bedrooms like breath on glass

Voice 1: We lay on our backs

                                          Voice 3: and listen

                                  Voice 7: The first humans are awake

Voice 6: farmers who dreamed of pulling on boots

Voice 5: wake and pull on mud-covered wellies

                                          Voice 7: Small children turn over

                              Voice 2: A barista flicks fag ash behind bins

Voice 1: Some people conduct other people

                                        Voice 3: like pipes carry sound

Voice 6: The old woman is like this

Voice 1: at night taxi drivers and foxes keep her awake

Voice 6: In the day

Voice 5: the whole wet town drains through her—

15

Voice 5 [channelling townspeople]: *house prices*

Voice 6 [channelling townspeople]: *this bloody weather*

Voice 5 [channelling townspeople]: *the state of this government*

Voice 1: grumbling inside her wrists

Voice 3: like damp gets into bones

Voice 5: This morning she is dozing in her chair

Voice 1: In her dream a cat she used to own pushes through the cat flap

Voice 5: steps out of her dream and circles her legs

Voice 6: sets to work washing the white fur around his paw

Voice 5: quite matter-of-factly

                                              Voice 7: the way ghosts do

                        Voice 8: And what about Michael?

Voice 5: Michael is still asleep

                        Voice 8: And inside his dreams?

Voice 1: Inside his dreams it's early summer

Voice 6: he kneels on the springy lawn outside his house

Voice 5: It needs a good mow

Voice 6: but first he needs to sharpen the mower blade

Voice 1: Here he is bent over

Voice 3: with his back to us

Voice 5: He is at the centre of a logical kingdom

Voice 6: garden hose neatly coiled

Voice 5: garage door freshly painted

Voice 1: hedge clipped at a clean bright angle

Voice 2: Sounds like Michael hasn't got much else to do

Voice 5: A typical boomer

Voice 2: a marigolds and Neighbourhood-Watch loser

Voice 1: What else does he have?

Voice 4 [channelling Michael like a seismometer translates tremors into the Richter scale]: I stupidly broke the lawnmower blade. Or rather, the blade has broken inside this chamber and got itself wedged. I can't get this stupid safety collar off. The clamp is fine. I can hear the catch inside click into place. I am having a nightmare because this stupid bloody guard is not fit for purpose. I think I can feel two raised bevels in the plastic but there's nothing to tell you what to do with them. If I pull lightly on the trigger, inside the noise of the blade is like a boot heel on scree, cracked flints in the gears. I haven't been to a mountain in a long time. No more tramping. No more diving off the path and keeping to the line of a hedge to get out into the fields. No nosing about in scree slopes for belemnites or wedges of slate that split under a chisel with a perfect

Voice 3: Like all old men

Voice 8: in his dream Michael is alive in two places at once

Voice 1: trying to break into a machine

Voice 3: that's not meant to open

Voice 5: Here he is kneeling on his lawn

Voice 6: pain flushing his kneecaps

Voice 6: His daughter has told him this

Voice 2: *repeatedly*

Voice 5: but he still grips the plastic

Voice 6: tries to force it apart

Voice 7: Here is Michael

Voice 1: bent over a lawnmower

Voice 6: at the exact same time

Voice 3: somewhere in the territory of his adolescence

Voice 1: he kneels on the side of a hill

Voice 7: there's an entire mountainside

Voice 8: alive inside this man

Voice 5: who can't quite seem to catch hold

Voice 6: of what's in front of him

black fern inside. The ground used to open itself to me like that. Going into the mouth of a cave and following it down until it was too small to walk, crawling until it was too tight to keep going on my hands and knees. Breathing air no one had breathed for a very long time if at all. And now I can't even get a removable cover off a damn lawnmower. How can it be for my safety if it won't let the bloody thing work? Half the instructions are in Chinese and the other half in French. When did French become the default! Who decided that? It's a sign of the times and it's a sign of what's going on with this government. All this compromise. All this giving away. I am a friendly person. I am happy to be part of a friendly nation. Friendly enough to let people learn our language. Friendly enough to let countries purchase our engineering. Our standards. Our systems of governing. Did you know India is the fourth largest economy and the biggest receiver of British aid? How did that happen? We don't even have a space program anymore. We are part of the EU space program! This damn plastic collar is exactly the problem. My daughter, she's always trying to teach me how these things work. A triangle on its side always means play. Two triangles fast-forward. Why not just write fast-forward? Just write what it is and let the damn thing be. She's always asking me questions: Are you drinking water? Why are you still smoking? Were you a happy child? A happy child? Well, I had a perfectly normal childhood. I had a dog, played cricket, failed my eleven plus and did woodwork at the thicko school. But look where I've been. Look where I have taken myself. No education, no

Voice 1: It's not a question of thrift

Voice 5: It's a question of principle

Voice 6: Look how it lights him from within
Voice 5: the difference

Voice 6: between what he wants

Voice 5: and what the world offers

Voice 1: ripping apart

Voice 3: like a thick scab from skin

Voice 8: This is not a memory

18

contacts, more often than not no dinner. I never had any safety guards. No plastic keeping my fingers safe but I got on with the job. And yes, I've lived one way and made sure she's lived another. There's no sadness in that. It's just history. Sometimes, I think she's afraid of the things that happened to me. But when you live up against it, you know who you are. I keep my fingers away from the blade because I know what will happen if my fingers slip. Isn't that better? Isn't that real? Not some safety label— the plastic, the EU, some set of internationally-agreed symbols. It is the same blade doing the same job with all this nonsense they've put around it that won't let me in. There are all these words around it. She has put all these questions around it. But it is the same simple thing at the centre it has always been. It's what they've put around it that is the problem. This stupid plastic collar that won't let me unhook my own damn clip and blade.

Voice 5: and when he touches the ground of his youth

Voice 6: watch how it unbuckles

Voice 5: mud eases apart

Voice 1: gifts him the perfect outline of a fern cast in stone

Voice 7: The whole hillside of his adolescence

Voice 6: held in a body that can't grasp this collar

Voice 5: and clip

Voice 1: It boils inside his body

Voice 6: the difference between the past

Voice 1: still alive inside him

Voice 6: and the present

Voice 1: a fury that pitches and foams

Voice 1: Look it spills out of his mouth

Voice 6: It scalds the ground

Voice 3: like hot water from a kettle

Voice 5: burning his own hands

Voice 1: splashes his daughter stood behind him

Voice 7: but each boiling drop

Voice 6: each moment of pain

Voice 1: is a way back into himself

Voice 2: back into the body

Voice 6: he was told

Voice 5: was his way into the world

Voice 1: the place where the whole world began

[*Lights down on Michael. Lights down on town. Chorus disperse like steam*]

Act One, Scene Three: Rain

[*The town in afternoon. A pub with a once blue carpet showing an Estonian stream of the game. In a road running off the High Street a woman parking her car, kids carrying in the Aldi shop. Dog walkers in the wet field throwing tennis balls from long plastic scoops. In the sandwich factory the afternoon shift spooning coleslaw onto buttered bread. Inside his house, an old man reading* The Daily Mail. *He shakes his head. He reaches for his tea. Chorus falling on windowpanes like heavy drizzle.*]

Voice 1: Some days the sky is so heavy with grey linen

Voice 3: it's hard to believe in the sun

Voice 6: Some days clouds unbutton themselves

Voice 5: over and over

Voice 6: across roof tiles and power lines

Voice 1: and we move so much like water

Voice 3: I begin to wonder if we are the rain

Voice 1: by which we mean

Voice 2: it's pissing it down

Voice 1: if we had skin we would be soaked to it

Voice 4 [stumbling like they've a bad headache]: Michael says *there's no such thing as bad weather just poor preparation*

Voice 6: Well Michael

Voice 2: lucky you

Voice 6: to have found yourself

Voice 5: always on the right side of a raincoat

Voice 4 [Still stumbling]: Michael says *luck doesn't come into it*

21

Voice 1: Here he goes again

Voice 2: like a pull-toy running down its string

Voice 1: He doesn't need to check he's been heard

Voice 6: just keeps speaking to the soaked air

Voice 3: moving his hands like he's signing to the deaf

Voice 4 [All Michael now]: Not one jot. Go outside on a day like today and look up at the sky: thick grey clouds horizon to horizon, no wind in the trees, no wind to rip clouds apart and let the light down and what that means is drizzle all day and if it's going to drizzle all day you've got options because it will settle on wool but not soak it and if you've not got wool a light rain jacket or parka or even a bloody bin bag will keep you perfectly dry but you do need something other than a hoody or T shirt and if you go out in one of those and get wet there's a lesson there and you can take advantage of it or not. At home my daughter and I sit on a sofa each to watch the news and one day there was a story about a holiday company collapsing and an interview with a woman outside a boarded-up branch and the reporter asked her *Are you feeling worried about what might happen to your holiday* and the woman says *Yes actually I am feeling quite worried about it all really* and then they cut back to the studio. Stop banging on about how you feel and do something about it! Get off your arse and bloody get out there! And my daughter said Dad! and I said What? Everyone's gone mad. It's all bonkers. Everyone's gone

Voice 6: not stopping

Voice 5: Why doesn't he stop for breath?

Voice 7: I used to think it was a kind of weaving

Voice 3: all this talking old men do

Voice 7: a kind of wax cloth

too far in the other direction. Then they went back to the headlines: the world is burning, a car company has put a car in space with a fake astronaut, footage from Syria and the Syria situation really made my blood boil because the first sign of   trouble I would be out. And she said You Have No Idea What You Would Do In That Situation but I do and I know what she would do too because while she insists the

Voice 3: spoken into being in pubs

Voice 2: in front rooms shouting at TVs

Voice 5: meant to cover their body from rain

22

world needs to be fair in her heart she's a winner. She got up and went out of the living room.

All men want to be free.

She went up to bed and then so did my wife and I sat up sleepless. I watched Question Time. Everything felt disconnected. Everything felt wrong. They kept asking the wrong questions like *Can you guarantee there will be no disruption in medicines* and some   old man saying We Will Be Fine There Are Still Rabbits In The Fields and Apples In The Trees and blitz spirit but that's not not what this is about. I don't actually even like the word Brexit. It's too flashy. I can't hear it without thinking of a Daily Mail headline and a photo of a Sweaty MP in the back of a car. How is this man from a cul-de-sac in Bournemouth going to survive on rabbits.

Everything felt wrong and disconnected because what this is really about is freedom. When my daughter graduated she said I Have Been So Lucky and I said Lucky? What's it got to do with luck. She worked like mad to get that degree but she said I've Been Very Privileged In How I Was Raised And Where I Was Born and I had to stop her there because she was born exactly where I wanted her to be. There's a 50- mile ring around London and if you're born in it you're 8 times more likely to have a degree and 15 times more likely

to be a home owner. That's not unfair, it's just a fact capital cities will be richer and you can look at that fact and act accordingly or not. I got up and out of what I was born into and I

Voice 7: Look how close it sits to his body

Voice 6: He really believes

Voice 5: all men are born in the same kingdom

Voice 6: the body a knowable country

Voice 5: where each man is king

Voice 6: when to live in this town

Voice 1: is to live in an aquarium of dirty water

Voice 3: they can't see beyond

Voice 7: He has inducted his daughter into this realm of the real

Voice 6: and hasn't he been a generous ruler?

Voice 1: Outside all this fuss about gender

Voice 6: treating her the same as his sons

Voice 7: but when she walks through the world he's given her

23

Voice 1: Look what it does to the light

chose to come down here and that kind of get up and go is what being British is all about and I refuse to be ashamed of it. If you went to the cinema when I was a child you'd see it – people being proud of who they are: films with British soldiers and British women doing interesting things but now it's either   American super heroes or kitchen sink dramas about dreary people who never do anything remotely worth watching. It's a dilution. It's a celebration of the average and I refuse to give way to the average when I've dragged myself out of it

Voice 6: doesn't it make it all seem real?

Voice 6: it bounces what little light the valley holds

Voice 5: back at him

Voice 7: This is the best chance he has at drying up any idea of luck

Voice 1: because luck isn't an inheritance that will keep her safe

And actually I don't care if there are distribution problems and I don't care if there are empty shelves because I would rather have nothing than rags on my back and a stick to shake than let these bastards win   I actually remember empty shelves I actually remember being out on the hill all day and making a tea out of   blackberries or bilberries or berries of some sort I forget the exact ones. And it was because there was nothing at home and learning you could manage in a jumper if it was drizzling if you ate your rasberries under the big tree and I wasn't scared then and I'm not scared now there's no reason to be.

Voice 7: Look at his body

Voice 8: lift these strips of skin to see what's underneath

Voice 6: Here

And she's wrapped up in this noise of news and nonsense that gets between her and the plain truth that each person is free to make what they want of life I made what I wanted out of my life and this is why people like us rise to the top   like two   corks straight

Voice 5: And here

to the

24

Voice 8: where his bicep and thighs once were

Voice 5: are all her choices
Voice 8: Watch
Voice 6: when she moves through his world
Voice 1: they twitch

Voice 3: like muscle fibres
Voice 7: And he's stood in the tent porch now
Voice 2: He's like Frankenstein's monster

Voice 6: stumbling out of the wet nylon
Voice 5: dragging his right foot forward to meet the left
Voice 1: stumbling out of his dreams

Voice 3: onto the moor

Voice 6: but look
Voice 5: as he staggers past
Voice 1: look at the places she's refused him
Voice 6: all the choices she's made
Voice 5: that say no to his world

Voice 1: It undoes the knots he's tied around his bones

Voice 6: It undoes the little engines
Voice 5: that drive his legs and arms
Voice 6: forward

Voice 7: This skin of words he's spoken into being

Voice 6: has kept him together
Voice 8: Watch him stumble to the bank-edge above the town now
Voice 1: Watch words spilling out of the townspeople's mouths

Voice 6: rise through the air

Voice 3: like fog

Townspeople [together]: *the will of the people!*

Voice 1: Whole sentences drift past roof tiles and treetops

Voice 7: reach out and touch them

Voice 8: hold them in your hands

Townspeople [together]: *a great union*

Voice 6: Words can hold anything you like

Voice 1: ideas
Voice 2: hot air

Townspeople [together]: *with a history to be proud of!*

Voice 7: anything that gives them weight enough

Voice 5: to chuck back and forth like bean bags

Voice 6: when you're bored

Voice 2: or scared

Townspeople [together]: *free to be fair and strong*

Voice 1: But when they reach him
Voice 6: out here on the moor
Voice 5: watch what they do to his body
Voice 1: They flush through his muscles and veins
Voice 6: organs and nerves

Voice 7: making his whole self ring
Voice 3: like a telephone call
Voice 1: through an empty house
Voice 6: and when the walls and ceilings of his body

Voice 3: shake like that

Voice 5: for the first time in years

Voice 1: isn't it a homecoming?

Voice 7: A return to his body

Voice 6: which yes

Voice 5: is a kind of truth

Voice 2: Oh Michael

Voice 1: living with words instead of skin

Voice 6: a country instead of an arm

Voice 5: dragging your right foot forward

Voice 1: to meet words that bring you back to yourself

Voice 5: What must to be yourself

Voice 1: though this skin you made

Voice 6: can't seem to keep out the rain

Voice 5: can't keep out a chorus who move

Voice 3: like rain

Voice 7: A soaked man

Voices [together]: insisting his dampness is a choice

[*Lights down on chorus. Lights down on town. Lights down on Michael.*]

27

Entr'acte

[Sounds of rain falling, stage in blackout. Spotlight up on Michael down-stage left. Michael's skin of words streaming out behind him in the wind. Some muscles missing. Some words ringing in his body like a telephone in an empty hall. Michael blinking and shielding his eyes as he looks into the audience.]

Michael:

I didn't know how to love my sons,
it was like trying to hold a plastic bag of water,
I'd go to plug one small rip and the whole thing
would collapse, I don't know what made me afraid.

She took the violence out of me the way
lightning rods draw damage from a storm,
the things she got up to— being cheeky to me,
getting drunk, coming back shoes in her hands.

She came to the home when mum died,
it's astonishing to watch your child pass exams,
learn to drive, take your phone from you
and say *No, Dad. How do you feel?*

Children are the most unreal real thing.

Dear god tell me it doesn't warp the metal
when it takes lightning from a storm.

[Michael blinking. Lights down. Rain sounds grow louder.]

29

Act Two, Scene 1: Evening

[A front room in early evening, a TV on in the corner. Woman on the sofa on her laptop. Teenager on the other sofa eating pasta from a bowl. Upstairs another teenager on his Xbox enters the lobby for a COD 4 Battle Royale. His friend comes online. The internet running like roots through the town carrying his smile through armoured cables. The town contracts. The town expands. The town, sick of waiting, turns over.]

[Chorus enter like low hanging cloud]

Voices [together]: There are worse things than being a chorus that moves

Voice 3: like water

Voices [together]: Sometimes we get under collars of raincoats

Voice 5: and ride the bus into town

Voice 6: hidden in nostrils and lungs

Voice 1: Yes there are worse things

Voice 6: than what rises from this town

Voice 1: worse things than a townspeople

Voice 6: dipping their bodies into a stream of language

Voice 1: to make the rooms of their life crash like cymbals

Voice 6: speaking themselves real with their fingers in their ears

Voice 7: There are worse things than ghosts

Voice 8: who get stuck up here like hefted ewes

Voice 7: men who don't know they're dead

Voice 1: Michael was always ruled by a consistent logic

Voice 6: he used his body and it grew tired

Voice 5: so he slept

Voice 6: When he was hungry he ate

Voice 1: and when his body was injured

Voice 6: on some rock or rough fence post

Voice 5: he packed the graze or flap of skin with Germolene

Voice 1: left his body to knit itself

Voice 5: back into one whole piece

Voice 7: Injury was something that happened from without

Voice 8: Other sorts of damage

Voice 7: kidney stones fibroids cancer

Voice 8: seemed faintly absurd

Voice 7: a peculiar thing to choose to do

Voice 1: Sometimes I feel sorriest for men

Voice 6: living on the rise of their bodies

Voice 1: believing they're permanent and real

Voice 7: trying to get back to the part of them

Voice 8: alive thirty forty years ago

Voice 7: bending to fix an unfixable mower

Voice 8: that no longer exists

Voice 7: because fury feels so much like youth

Voice 1: I feel sorry for Michael

Voice 6: organising love like it's a logical process

Voice 5: a question of cause and effect

Voice 6: like the engine in a car

Voice 5: in a garage where his wife and bored children

Voice 6: have to stand around

Voice 1: nodding and smiling to his monologue of fixing

> Voice 7: living quiet lives

> Voice 8: outside the bright centre of attention

> Voice 7: where he worked alone

Voice 2: It must have been impossible to hear anything

Voice 6: as he climbed from pistons into:

Voice 4: *these damn spark plugs   these bloody foreign cars   what this country needs*

Voice 6: in three easy steps

Voice 1: Almost impossible to hear

Voice 6: over the sound of his muscles ringing like telephone calls

Voice 1: a dark spot of cells

Voice 6: nestled in the loop of his guts

Voice 5: dividing and doubling

> Voice 7: Why bother with the quiet column of your body

> Voice 8: when you can flush it with borrowed sound

> Voice 7: His daughter does it too look

Voice 1: here she is fifty miles to the West in a big northern city

Voice 6: where they hang red lanterns in trees for Lunar New Year

Voice 1: She slots her body into a protest

Voice 6: The crowd pitches and foams

Voice 1: shouts slogans

Voice 6: carries funny signs

Voice 8: What does she want?

Voice 6: Who has time to answer this question?

Voice 1: Who has time for questions at all

Voice 6: when there is all this energy

Voice 1: running through her body

Voice 5: what some people call virtue

Voice 6: some people fury

Voice 1: lighting her up

Voice 5: like a mobile phone

Voice 7: It feels like a path through

Voice 8: feels like truth

Voice 7: and is

Voice 8: although not in the way she expects

Voice 1: Look here is Michael's sister now

Voice 6: on the other side of the town

Voice 5: sat at her dining room table

Sylvia [writing]: … if you're lucky you fall quickly into the ruins of your body. As my husband left slowly (it took years) it broke me open like the back of a spoon on an egg, the pain of no longer being beautiful, no longer being young undoing my breasts and hair until I had nothing left to keep me up. I fell into being a person again. Sat on the floor of my life like a child, a bit fat and quite drunk on my own

expensive wine, totally free from being a creature that's born the moment it's seen...
[At the desk Sylvia smiling and taking a sip of wine]

Voice 1: Michael's daughter has felt this

Voice 5: moving about in the roots of herself

Voice 6: felt herself begin to fall out of girlhood

Voice 1: slipping her body into a protest crowd

                                        Voice 7: or the night her grandma died

              Voice 8: I hold it out to you this moment of falling

Voice 6: Here are Michael and his daughter driving all night to get home

Voice 5: They arrive at 4am and sit in the car

                                        Voice 7: A full moon is setting over the house

Voice 1: Tiredness washes through them

Voice 6: no space for anything else

Voice 5: not sadness not love
                                        Voice 7: no language or history

Voice 1: only the fact of two exhausted bodies

Voice 6: sharing the same carful of air

                        Voice 7: There are moments inside us the dead never leave

              Voice 8: but stay waiting to be needed

Voice 6: Maybe we make all this noise
                                        Voice 7: all this fixing and fury

Voice 5: because it's the only thing

Voice 6: that can hold these silences

Voice 5: The dearest things in our life

Voice 1: though we are not quite sure they really did happen

                Voice 8: I hold it out to you this moment in the car

Voice 1: before they sigh and undo their seatbelts

Voice 6: open their doors and climb back into their lives

Voice 5: dipping their bodies into streams of words

Voice 6: that flow out from his newspaper her Netflix specials

Voice 1: The stories they told themselves

Voice 6: and told about each other

Voice 5: living their lives back to back

              [Chorus exit like water draining through old pipes.
         Lights fade on the car centre-stage. Blackout. Curtain.]

Acknowledgements

This pamphlet was written as part of my PhD research at The Centre for New Writing, The University of Manchester. Huge thanks are due to the staff and students at the Centre, especially to Rebecca Hurst, Fatema Abdoolcarim and Usma Malik for their input on the text, as well as their personal love and support. I also owe a huge thank you to my supervisor Vona Groarke who oversaw this project from start to finish and to my PhD examiners John McAuliffe and Jane Draycott. Many thanks also to the School of Arts, Languages and Cultures for the 3-year research grant which made this piece financially possible.

Enormous thanks are also due to my research collaborator Pablo de Orellana whose work on the New Right and aesthetics has so informed this piece's composition. I am also so grateful to Kings College London for the residency which allowed me to work on this pamphlet further.

To my family, especially my husband Paul and daughter Iris, thank you for everything.

[Chorus lay out their unrest]